D1825506

NOT MUCH
RHYMES WITH
CANCER

NOT MUCH RHYMES WITH CANCER

A BOOK OF HEALING POEMS

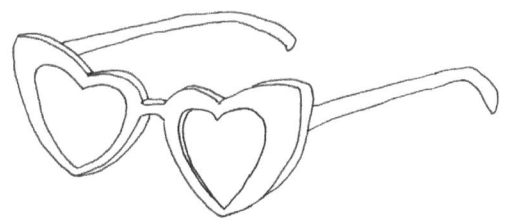

by

EMILY THOMAS

VALLEY PRESS

First published in 2024 by Valley Press
Woodend, The Crescent, Scarborough, UK, YO11 2PW
valleypressuk.com

ISBN 978-1-915606-54-9
Cat. no. VP0244

Copyright © the estate of Emily Thomas 2024

All rights reserved. No part of this publication may be
reproduced, stored in or introduced into a retrieval system,
or transmitted in any form, by any means (electronic,
mechanical, photocopying, recording or otherwise) without
prior written permission from the rights holders.

Illustrations by Megan Williams.
Cover design by Charlotte Thomas-Hui.
Interior design by Jamie McGarry.

Contents

Foreword
by Lee Thomas

"I am not above, but all around you like a glove."
– Emily Thomas, née Brooks

"Don't cry because it's over, smile because it happened."
– Not Em's words, though definitely her outlook

The moment I met Em, outside a Sainsbury's in Balham, I knew she was special.

She was special before cancer.

The most sunny of sunshine souls, deeply thoughtful, immeasurably selfless. Effortlessly trendy, utterly hilarious.

The bestest of BFFs. Devoted daughter, supportive sister, adoring auntie, wonder wife and mega mum.

A soul that radiated positivity and fun like no other. If you knew her, the mere mention of her name and the sides of your mouth would involuntarily curl into a smile, as you recounted that unmistakable, inimitable laugh.

A shy, modest and unassuming soul who was more often than not both the funniest and the smartest person in the room, though she would never, ever think that of herself.

An accomplished marketing strategist, performance grade pianist, secret shower singer and the fanciest of fancy dress creators.

A new mum who relished every moment of pregnancy and motherhood. Our little boy Griff was her world. Em's default Happy setting was already at a 10. When Griff arrived he cranked it up to 11.

Cancer didn't define her. Though in some way it ignited something inside her. A confidence to think "F**k it" and to find time for the important things that busy everyday life detracts from.

In just 18 months Em achieved things that many people would be happy to achieve in a lifetime; spurred on by, not constrained by her diagnosis.

The mental strength and heart to do this blew us all away on a daily basis. Every day I felt I was the luckiest man alive to have this force of nature, this embodiment of positivity and gratitude, in both Griff's and my life.

She spent that time, showing by example, how to deal with adversity and how to live with a permanent "glass half full" attitude.

What made our Em all the more remarkable, genuinely inspirational, is how her lust for life changed when we received the earth-shattering news of Em's secondary breast cancer.

It didn't change one little bit, not a jot. What should have been an incessant living hell, was abundantly populated with laughter, creativity, family time, selfless acts of fundraising, research, raising awareness of secondary breast cancer and supporting and coaching a community of people that we now found ourselves an active part of.

She reignited a passion for words that had remained dormant since age nine, when she had her first poem published, 'Pollution', in a book called *Through the Hoop*:

Big chimneys everywhere,
Pouring smoke into the air
Lots of rubbish at my feet
When I walk down my dusty street.
People dumping oil in the sea
Oh dear! What a catastrophe
CFCs spilling chemicals into the air
Soon gas masks on,
So be aware.

A spark soon became a wildfire. (Em never did anything by half and was annoyingly good at everything she turned her hand to.)

Em found words healing, she wrote beautifully. Em was all about the now, "it's the only moment that ever truly exists" she would say, "be in it, live it, love it ... be present, don't watch it through a phone when you're actually there".

Em's poetry wouldn't always be about positivity and hope, she also dealt with the anguish, uncertainty and guilt which came with such a diagnosis. I could see first-hand how Em's creative candour was a healing means of expressing herself, a cathartic release, every time pen touched paper.

The response to Em's words was incredible. People who felt that they were going through this alone and that no one else thought and felt like they did suddenly realised they *weren't* alone. There were others just like them, who shared their experiences, people who could understand them, who were willing to help them. People who would now also find comfort in reading and writing too. Em set up the Naked Poets with her great mate Tracey, organising workshops for other people with cancer to use words as their escape. To hear people say at the end of their events that they never thought anything positive could come from their diagnosis was moving beyond words.

Our mission is to share Em's poetry as far as we possibly can, and the book you have in your hands is one way that we'll do that. Thank you for supporting this.

There's an unfillable hole in Em's family and friends' lives. We no longer see her with our eyes, but we'll never stop feeling her in our hearts.

She's no longer encumbered by the constraints of her physical form, and some of the shitty bits which come with that. Instead, she's everywhere, she's wild, she's free.

Who better to express what's contained in the pages that follow than Em herself. Taken from her very first post on her Insta channel @notmuchrhymeswithcancer:

"This is a collection of poems written from diagnosis of stage IV breast cancer to present day. In parts it's an outpouring of emotion, a place to vent and expel negative thoughts. Mostly it's a tale of hope, positivity and gratitude.

It's helping me and I hope it might help others too. Em."

If you or someone you care about has been diagnosed with cancer, please visit macmillan.org.uk/cancer-information-and-support for help and resources.

"Poetry is thoughts that breathe and words that burn."
– Thomas Gray

SELF

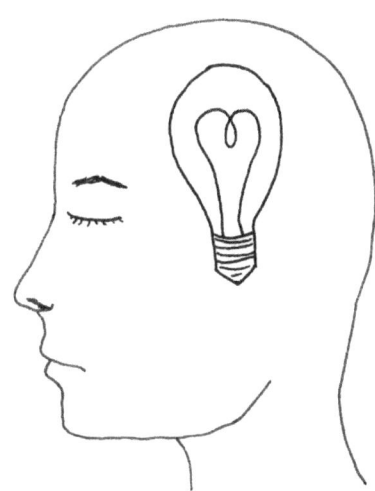

*Through our experience
we're united but our stories
are unique.*

*Was I that out of sync with my own body,
that I didn't notice it was out of tune?*

*Cancer has turned a light on
and revealed myself.*

*Having a ponder what it's gonna
feel like to be a one-tit wonder...*

I'm a real poet now

Finally, I have arrived!
I am perching on a velvet chair
in a coffee shop window
writing this poem

Poetry books to my right
Ginger tea to my left

The ideas are sure to come
The flood is about to begin
I've just got to be patient

Ooh, chocolate avocado cake!

Right, I must start to write
But what to write about?

The snaking students queue for Greggs next door?
The man who just fell into his phone?
The boy from school that's sat behind me
who I haven't said hello to
because his eyes will say
"Why doesn't she have any hair?"

Face

A weathered face
Battered and cracked
Like a broken pot

Lines map a story
But need to be filled
Maybe, one day, with gold

Body

Body reclaimed
Picked up
Like driftwood
Made into art

My Hair Then

When it came to my hair
Why did I care?

If I'd been more brave
I'd have held a bald rave
If I hadn't worried for others
Hid head under covers
If I'd left scarves on their peg
Knitted cosies for my egg

Then all of those days
I'd have been soaking up rays

My Hair Now

When it comes to my hair
I really don't care

If it suits me a lot
The colour and crop
If I can carry it off
My semi-thatched loft
If it wouldn't suit you
Not something you'd do

If that's all that you see
Know there's much more to me

Chasing

I need to stop
chasing life.
It's right here
in front of me.

Tinted

If I looked in the mirror through
pink heart sunglasses,
would I love myself more?

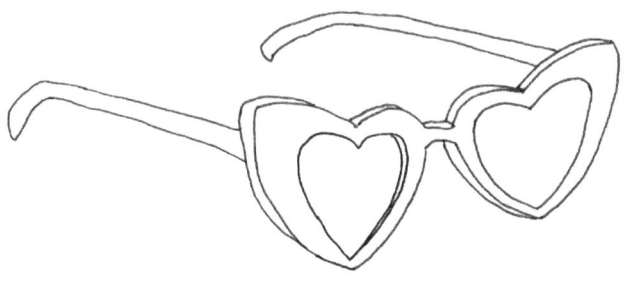

My Body

My body needs some kindness,
A warm hand on my heart
My body needs compassion,
A chance to hit restart

My body needs a polish,
Deep within each cell
My body needs nourishing food,
To make and keep it well

My body needs expansive energy,
A golden ray of light
My body needs hands that heal,
To help to put things right

My body needs to move,
To dance and jump and shake
My body needs to be calm,
With meditation when I awake

My body needs positivity,
To get through when things go wrong
My body needs confidence,
A mind that's firm and strong

Identity

Cancer makes you question your identity
And I've got a LOT of questions

Am I still me?
Is there an "old" me and a "new" me?
Do I still want to be the "old" me?
Can I even remember the "old" me?
Do I have to have a "new" me?
What does "new" me look like?
What could "new" me look like?
Who am I?

Answers to follow.

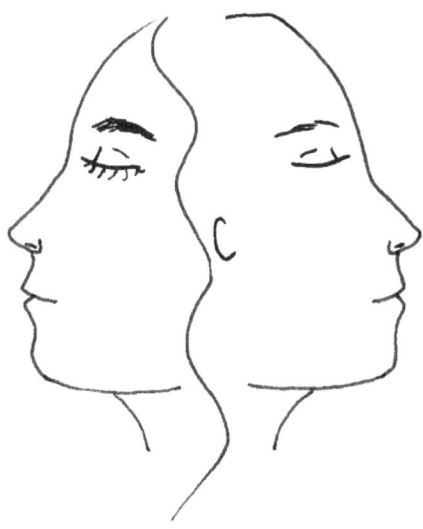

Back to the Heart

It's noisy out there
But then
It's also noisy in here
In my mind

In searching for proof
Where is MY truth?

Out there
there's a thousand
stories and opinions
In here,
there's a thousand
stories and opinions

I'm looking for what sticks
The candle to my wick

I'm a magpie
for miracles
But then trail
other realities

It's time to turn in
Avoid the spin

Just return to the start
Go back to my heart

LOVE AND GRATITUDE

My heart is full of love
And my body is full of life.

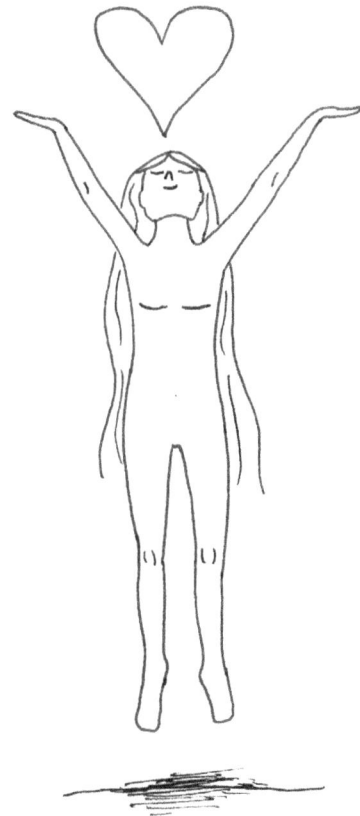

A Love Letter to My Body

Body, I'm here
Can you hear me?
You might not recognise me
I'm louder than before

Body, I know
we've not always been close
There's been some dissonance
despite being written on the same page

But I know you more than ever now

You're not an ornament,
you're a library of self-expression
You're not an object for self-loathing
you're worthy of worship

You're not just a machine,
you're entwined with nature
You're not autonomous,
you're only whole with mind and soul

This past year, we've grown so much closer

We've created new life with science
and delivered the most precious gift
We've weathered an uncontrolled storm
and dissipated it to nothing

I can hear what you're saying to me now

Body, thank you
From the bottom of our heart
Thank you.
I love you.

Powerful Love

Your love powers me on,
Sparking joy
And bringing strength
To sometimes gloomy realities

Your love turns on the lights
Of life
And lets them brightly shine
So that they burn with hope

Without your love,
The days would be dark
And moments of fault
Difficult to weather

Wonder Women

My wonder women have my back
There for me when I start to crack

Committed to looking after me
Medicine, food and spirituality

Helping me find strength and my truth
A healing lasso, I'm living proof

My cheerleaders, my teachers
My guides, my treaters

I'm forever grateful for all that you do
My wonder women, I love you!

Little Frog

It was a new morning in May
When you swam into this world
Fresh and long-limbed
Eyes staring up at us,
Dark like marbles
Skin new,
Wrinkled like a prune
Away from your hushed hibernation
Bewildered by the brightness
You slowly gazed around the room
With sweet staccato croaks
New life on a new morning in May
Our little baby frog

First Touch

Waves brought you to shore,
brought you gliding
into the outside world,
into my hands
Nets made of cashmere
softly bringing you to safety
Bringing the smoothest stone
from the roughest sea
A mother's pearl, offered
by silken water rainbows
Offered like a tiny glistening
fresh full moon

First touch
First skin on skin
Son on mother
Mother on son

Lee-monade

"When life gives you lemons,
surround yourself with great fruit pickers."

We're deep deep diving
Drinking it up and thriving
We're sucking out the sour
Taking in every hour
We're crushing up each lemon
Often in quick succession
We're keeping ourselves sharp
Fresh brightness in the dark
You're our lemon farmer
The sweetest husband and father

We love you Lee.

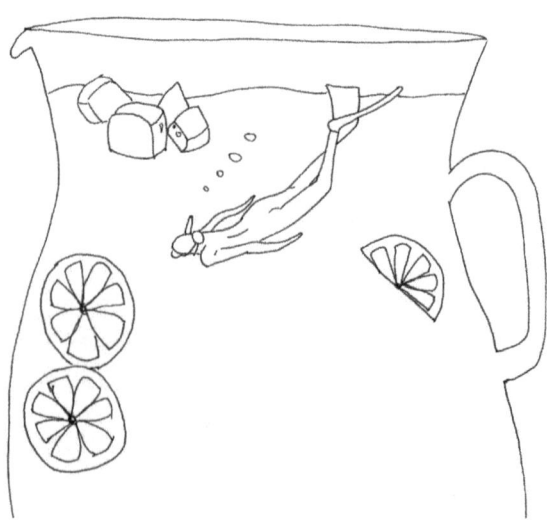

Museum

Things I'll put in my museum –
My love for you.
The only story that needs preserving.

CHANGE

You are an uninvited guest.
Or did I invite you in some way?

Feeling through the fog to find a
clearing where I can breathe.

Our stories are ours to write
With the words that we choose.

Paper Thin

This skin I'm in
Feels paper thin
It used to withstand so, so much
But now cracks and breaks,
With the slightest touch

Blank

Frozen moments
Staring into space
No past, present or future
As blank as walls

A short history of me and you (my left boob)

Begging you to bloom while my friends made friends with their blossoming bosoms. Wondering when I could wear a bra (can you wear a training bra with no boobs?!) You finally arriving (hoorah!) but feeling funny in school jumpers. Huddling you under a Topshop paisley pink handkerchief top and countless other slithers of satin. Popping you in a denim bustier (paired with jeans, *Bewitched* style). The never-ending quest for the perfect strapless bra. Never really knowing your true size (do any bras actually fit?!) Thinking you belonged to the male gaze. Giving you to the male gaze. Reeling from rhetoric that bigger was better. Feeling like you were inferior to others. Landing on bralets for comfort and convenience. Nuzzling my newborn close to you in the birthing pool and in the sanctuary of night. Cloaking you with savoy cabbage leaves to soothe "engorgement". Being poked, prodded and punctured to find out what the lump was. Calling you my useless left tit (ULT). Not being able to even look at you. Throwing treatment at you. Making friends again with you.

Note: I don't believe it was engorgement, and it certainly wasn't just engorgement. It was my body crying out that something was seriously wrong. It was only when I gave up feeding on my left breast that it was clear there was a lump that wasn't going away. More education for midwives and lactation experts is needed, as well as more education for women to question symptoms (it might not be pregnancy related), advocate for themselves and seek a second, third, fourth opinion.

Mastectomy Musings

Without my left boob
  my heart is closer
    to the sun, moon and stars

Healing Spa

Comfy chair
Massage for my hair
Tea on tap
Book on lap
Heated cushions and a blanket
A trolley with a banquet
Reclining back to relax
Drifting in and out of naps
Friendly faces
Community spaces
It could be a spa trip away –

But it's treatment day

Chemo

A thick, heavy blanket
creeps around my body
Holding me down,
suffocating normality

The metallic buzz
hums around every cell
Lead weights,
make me sluggish and slow

I drag myself
through the dense forest
Clawing for the way out
Holding the light that's in sight

Uninvited Guest

And from seemingly nowhere
you made your grand entrance
Peacocking around my body
Loud, proud
Bold, brilliant
Secret, sly

A master of disguise
Sinister in the shadows
Guest of honour at
a masquerade ball
How long had you been hiding?
Leaching goodness

How dare you have been
dancing near my cub
That was one step too far

He never liked you
He gave me clues
He pulled off your mask

Bliss interrupter
Quietness disrupter
Joy snatcher
Sleep not, rest up
Your partying days are over

Scan Results Day

Sitting in the waiting room
Time stops still

My terror masked by a smile
My pounding heart hushed by small talk

Then everything changes
"A spectacular and truly remarkable
response"

A face flooded with joyful tears
My body vibrating with disbelief

Sitting in the oncologist's office
Time restarts

My Dress But Different

Dress alterations are now in full swing
Snip, stitch and zhoosh to get rid of the cling
Many a good time we had together
Now it bunches and pulls more than ever

Some parts to be kept, they're too good to lose
How much to change? Should it still match the shoes?
What kind of dress would now suit my new life?
Mirror reflection, the joy and the strife

Maybe splashed florals that dance in the light
Floaty and free, lift me day into night
Wishing well buttons set it off a treat
Clasping me, holding me if off my feet

All frills removed as well as the old lace
Fierce structure and folds to sit in their place
A new zip snaps shut the previous frock
Tweaking the new one, then ready to rock

Levitate

Waves chase waves

Foot to head

Floating cells

Ribbon veins

Notes hit notes

Scale my spine

Body on

Shivers soar

Levitate

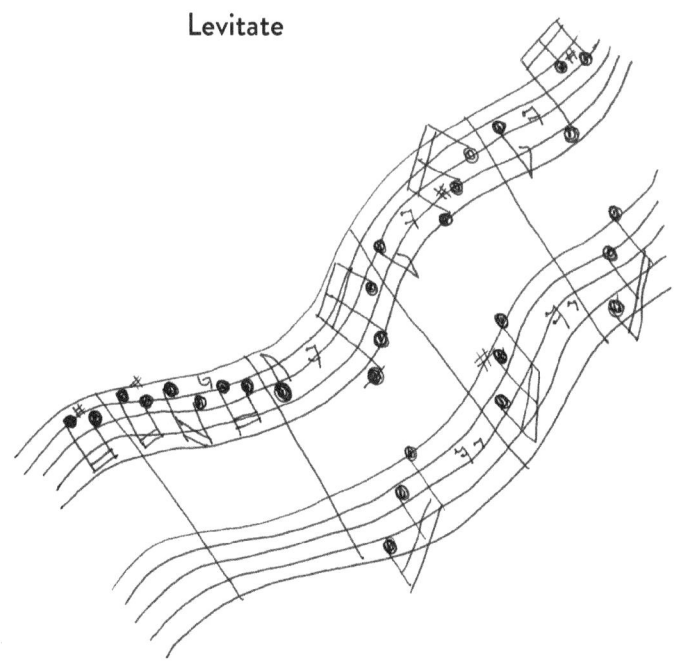

Ocean

A poem about pulsatile tinnitus

There's a mighty ocean in my ears
Singing to the rhythm of my heart

Are those strata sounds to soothe me?
Rocking serenity into my soul?

Waves roll on and on, on repeat
Crashing to steady shoreline

Whispers turn to loud growls
Wind driving clockwork conditions

Am I missing the message?
Is that a bottle bobbing on the horizon?

A devoted heart on a pilgrimage
Intrepid explorer in the wilds

Do you want to take me back home?
Are you happier in my head?

Mother Nature brings no bitterness
So for now I'll swim in your greatness

FEAR

You were very good at hiding.
Could I have been better at seeking?

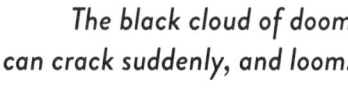

The black cloud of doom
can crack suddenly, and loom.

Uninvited Guest Too

So, you're back at the party
Uninvited
Turns out you were hiding
Hiding in the shadows
Of my mind

You're just a hanger on
A leftover
I was pretty surprised
To see you
You of all things

I'm afraid you're not welcome
Not on the guest list
Not a plus one
Not invited
You need to leave

Stuck

The words "I'm afraid it's
not good news"
Echo in my head on repeat
The stylus on the record of my
diagnosis, stuck
Going round and around and around and around

It haunts my mind with an unearthly
memory
That seems so surreal yet real
An out of the body experience,
the words dancing around me,
Inviting a reaction

The physical moment has long passed
But the mental image holds strong
Every look, every word, every move
Defining and shaping a moment that
would change my life forever

And now the words hang in my mind
Left blowing in a changing breeze
Wondering if they should cling on
Or blow away in the winds of the future

Take Me

Take this
Take that
Take it now
Take it next
Take it in the morning
Take it at night
Take with food
Take without food
Take to survive
Take to thrive
Take, take, take
Taking its toll

Falling

My foot slips
Unstable rock
I'm falling,
falling fast

Sharp rocks,
slice me
Boulders,
bruise me

Scrambling
Tumbling
Grasping
Gasping

Still, for a moment
Safe on a ledge
Until it breaks.
I'm falling again

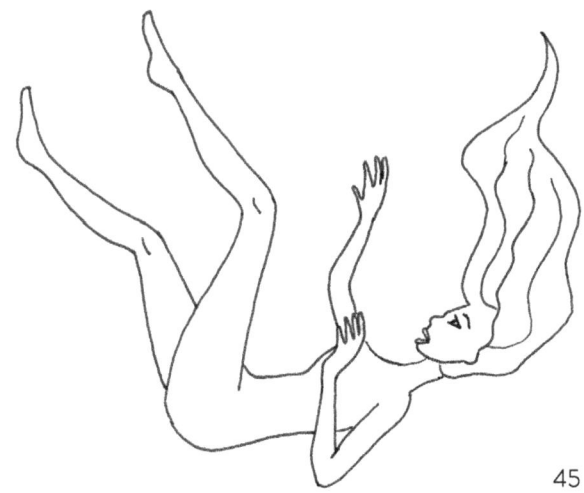

Guilt

Gut-wrenching guilt
Crawls through my body
Slowing taking over
Crescendoing into panic

Could I have prevented it?
Could I have spotted it sooner?
Was I blinkered by breastfeeding?
Was I even thinking about my own health?

My rational mind
Knows I did everything I could
My emotional mind
Has other ideas

An unforgiving wave
Crashing over and over
Then the calm comes
Stillness before the next storm

Anxiety

One thousand tap dancing mice. A zipped up sleeping bag made of cotton wool. Glazed-over gazing at a TV show called life. An acid house kaleidoscope on the back of my eyelids. Clambering up a rocky cliff. Bambi on ice, wearing rollerskates. Knee deep in molasses mud, in a deserted field. Cells like unherded sheep. A runaway, rickety rollercoaster. The play button taped down in musical statues. A jumpsuit made of wasps.

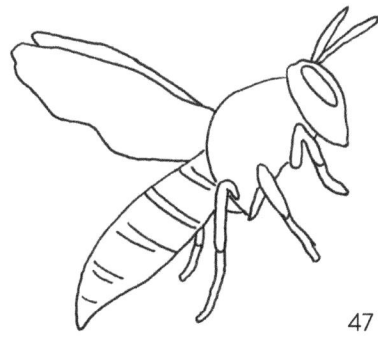

Reminder

A reminder to my mind.
Do one.

HOPE

How can something so grounding
make me feel like I'm flying?

Darkness will fall but light will
always follow.

Wrap me up and hold me tight, with a
golden thread of hope and light.

New adventure brings new hope.

Hope

All you need is hope.
Story-sharing,
future-glimmering,
bucket-filling
hope.

Hibernation

Outside the window
The humming delivery bikes
Break the silence of the streets
And signal another lockdown

Inside, I hibernate
Tucked away from the world
Cotton wool walls
Providing a protective cocoon

While moments are missed
Time and space is created
To rest and repair
To be grateful and grow

Healing Rainbow

Healing rainbow
Take off in flight
Fill my head
With healing light

Shiny ball
Of rainbow glow
Fill my head
With truth I know

Bright lights seep
Into every cell
Fill my head
And make it well

Colours flood
To my core
Fill my head
Just like before

Breathe

Dam breaking breath.
Unstoppable force that
fractures stillness

Rapids of stale air cascade
from every pore, escaping
with feral abandonment

Jet streams and rosy clouds
collide. Drifting off
to the hopeful beyond

Magic Beans

Each morning I count
out my magic beans
Glossy and glittering,
the stuff of dreams

Down the pills go
Down, down the hatch
Plant them in my body
My terrain, my patch

Minerals, vits, herbs
Pink, yellow and blue
Sending with them
A healing wish or two

Heartbroken

And then my heart
fell to the floor
Shattering into
a thousand pieces

Each helpless piece
weary, marooned,
blinking back at me,
searching for answers

My shipwrecked heart,
lost at sea
Treasured shards
waiting to be rescued

But slowly, a shine
and glimmer
Drifting back
to life

Slowly, a stitch
back together
Golden threads
of hope and love

The Campfire

At the peak of the hill
A roaring campfire
Embracing the night's chill
Inviting spirits higher
We clamber to the top
Find sanctuary, to stop.

Sacred sparks of sunshine
Soaring into the air
Fireflies holding truths
Fear and hope laid bare
Campfire words float by
Kissing the shifting sky

Lives different but the same
Pictures in a locket
Silent echoing notes
Hidden, scrunched, in pockets
Talking into the night
Often no words in sight.

*Inspired by summer holiday campfires, which led to synergies
with the wonderful secondary breast cancer community.
Right by each other's sides, every step of the way. Inspiring,
sharing, supporting, praying, hoping.*

Cobwebs

Autumn leaves
drift away
like dusty cobwebs
in the wind

RESILIENCE

Realising you have control, gives you freedom.

Statistics do not define us.
We define the statistics.

I'm steadying the ship
that sails upon the rough seas of my mind.

You've locked me in
a cage but the key is within reach.

Wild Woman

I'm leaving my lair. I'm running into
the storm. Ditching the umbrella.
Letting the hail smash against my skin.
I'm welcoming the wind as it whips
around my naked (egg) head. I'm soaking
up the sun (safely!) Sprinting into
the freezing sea. Foraging in the
forest. I'm sticking my feet deep, deep
into the earth. I'm letting the fire
burn, burn, burn.

I'm letting the wildness in.
And letting the wildness out.

The Last Moment

Before going into a scan

A warm breeze
sweeps over my face
Autumn sun
soaking into my skin

Hazy lavender
sways softly
Conducted by
batons of buds

The hum of bees
vibrates in the air
Soothing my
thumping heart

Faces emerge from
the dark cave
Happy and relieved
Sad and destroyed

Nature quietens
the terror
The last moment
before the noise

Nocturne

I'm asleep
but you're awake.
You're awake
in my body
when I'm awake and
when I'm asleep.
Really, you should
be asleep
when I'm asleep and
when I'm awake.

You must be
tired?
Tired of the
blue bottle buzz buzz
buzzing around my brain
and my body,
my body is tired
of no golden silent
shut eye
or serenity.

Are you afraid
of the dark?
Does darkness falling
make you move
into molasses darkness
or falter your mood?
Know there's a lightness
coming behind you
to show you
the way out.

Useless Left Tit (ULT)

I should've known
You'd be the bit
To f**k things up
Turn all to s**t

Remember that time
You were so engorged
Cold showers, cabbage leaves
Tactics we forged

You always played second
Fiddle to right
Who did most of the feeding
All day and all night

And now you're back
With a whacking great lump
Masked by pregnancy and nursing –
So I'm in a right grump!

But let's go on
This journey together
And try to become friends again
Forever and ever

Tamoxifen Tears

Here comes the rain
Pouring down my face
Uncontrollable flood
Let it flow, let it flow
Then they go

Pillow

Scream into the pillow
Let the feathers
Soak up your tears
Then plump yourself up
And keep going

Let it Go

A jack-in-the-box voice
sabotaging self-belief
Just let it go

A trip and slip into
sliding door what-ifs
Just let it go

A fireball of fear
dragon deep
Just let it go

A murky sludgy swamp
of rancid thoughts
Just let it go

A longing for longer
instead of the now
Just let it go

A not-enough needle
stuck on repeat
Just let it go

A search for "purpose"
that's under my nose
Just let it go

A cage of shooting stars
scrambling to fly
Just let it go

Just.
Let.
It.
GO

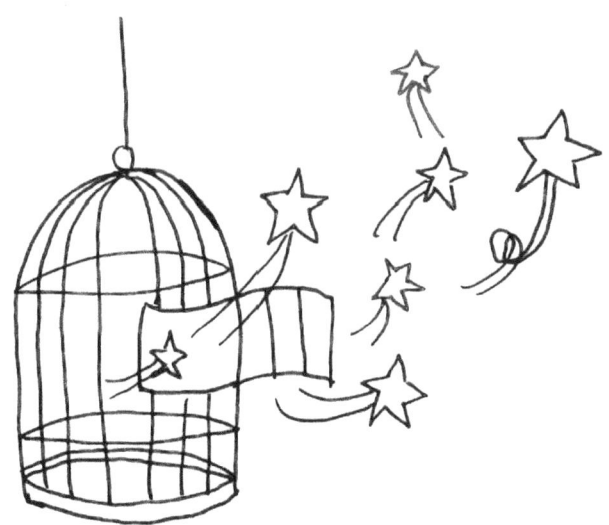

What the...

Sometimes I think
what the actual f**k

Then I take a deep breath
and move on

BELIEF

*I believe to the centre of my core
that my body can heal just like before.*

*I'm believing big.
As big as I possibly can that
anything is possible.*

*Whole-hearted
Gut-warming
Belief-building
Trust*

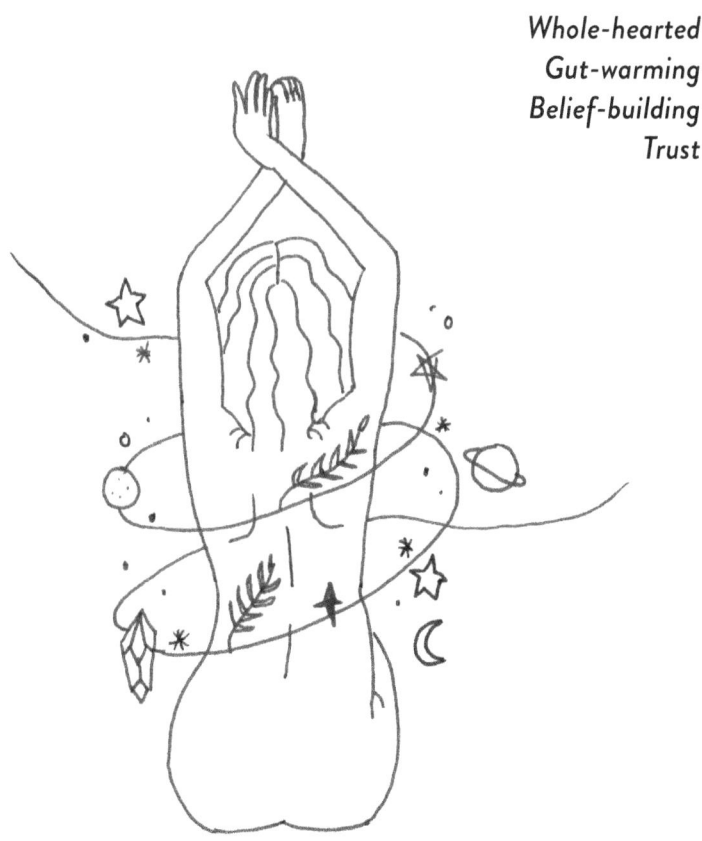

A Goodbye Letter

So, this is goodbye. Adios, ciao, hwyl
fawr. How should I say goodbye?
No *see you later alligator*; our relationship is
snapping shut. A full stop. Not a comma;
no connection needed. I guess we'll
always have London; acquainted with the
warm lavender waiting; sad eyes staring
but hazy hope unfolding (what a time that
was!) No *sweet sorrows here*, only Jelly
Tots joy of our parting (which reminds
me, I've hidden all the sugar). So
perhaps it's our fairytale ending? It's
certainly been a page turner, but you
could really do with peppering in some
humour – have you thought about writing
classes? One to consider.

Anyway, you know Dr Seuss says "Don't cry
because it's over, smile because it
happened"? Well, I am smiling. But it's
no half-time orange smile. This one is
sucked and dry; left on the pitch at the
end. I did hear your *so long partner* but
it kind of made me wince; you've played
with me to death! Well not quite, but I'm
definitely chipped and worn. Somewhere in
this letter is gritted-teeth gratitude.
And that's about all you're getting. I
hope you enjoy your relocation but don't
leave your address. I won't need to
contact you.

Don't Forget the Fun

A life-changing diagnosis
With serious doctor faces,
Sad and sorry eyes
Understanding and processing.
Planning and researching.
Surviving –

But don't forget the fun.

A life-loving dance
With my husband in the kitchen,
Happy and grateful smiles
Prancing and cavorting,
Singing and laughing.
Thriving.

Less or More

You could say that cancer takes away
And leaves you with less
Less certainty
Less health
Less time
Less life

But cancer can
Give you more

More clarity
More gratitude
More love
More life

So, I'm still me
But more me

Metamorphosis

The caterpillar
Moved through life
Head down, busy
With furry blinkers on

The butterfly
Soars high
In glorious freedom
Finally able to see clearly

Sunshine

Lying starfish on the grass,
gorging on golden goodness

that polishes and shines
my dampened body and mind

Hazy rays reaching
and stretching into every cell

as they propel me from one
sunshine thought to another

Bones warmed, head hugged,
face freckled, body embraced,

safety, from certainty,
that the sun will shine again.

THE UNIVERSE

I'm building a galaxy from healing stars

Stardust

Every prayer and blessing
of hope to get well
Is a shot
of healing stardust
to each and every cell

Vibrations

Emily placed a huge amount of importance on positive energy, positive thought and setting positive intentions – reclaiming joy, freedom and life.

Buzz
Buzz
Buzz

Vibrate with love
Vibrate with gratitude
Vibrate with compassion

Buzz
Buzz
Buzz

Raise your energy
Raise your vibrations
Raise your attraction

Buzz
Buzz
Buzz

Reclaim joy
Reclaim freedom
Reclaim life

Buzz.

Lucky Number 14

Never had a lucky number
Never one of note
But now the number 14
Is one on which I dote

A shiny new collection
Upon the charm bracelet of life
Special number 14s
Moments of joy after strife

My one true love's birthday
Falling in bright September
A time of shifting colours
A diagnosis to remember

Our precious baby's welcome,
Entering the world that day,
After a long, long journey
He sprang into life in May.

The day of my first scan results –
No evidence of disease
No sign of it left in my body
Making me weak at the knees

Today is also a special day
A new moon, a solar eclipse
A turning point for big changes
New beginnings upon my lips

My charm bracelet is heavy
With gratitude and joy
Shine bright, number 14s
There's love and life to enjoy

You Glow Girl

Our bodies' trick?
We're a giant glow stick.
The body literally
glimmers.
We shine
brightest
when we're burning
the most energy.

The energy we burn
makes us an upside-down
glow worm;
head-first,
which doesn't seem
that surprising
given the
circus
in many of
our minds.

How magical
to think
we can emit a beautiful
luminosity,
send radiant beams
into the world.

We are fluorescent,
bioluminescent.
We are fireflies,
attracting others' eyes.

You glow girl.

Light up

Cells switch on like cabochons –
                        metronomic waves of light

Searchlight

Body searchlight, illuminate the skies –
                Funnel for falling stardust

Fireflies

Freckles fade to fireflies –
                sparks a cosmic cha-cha-cha

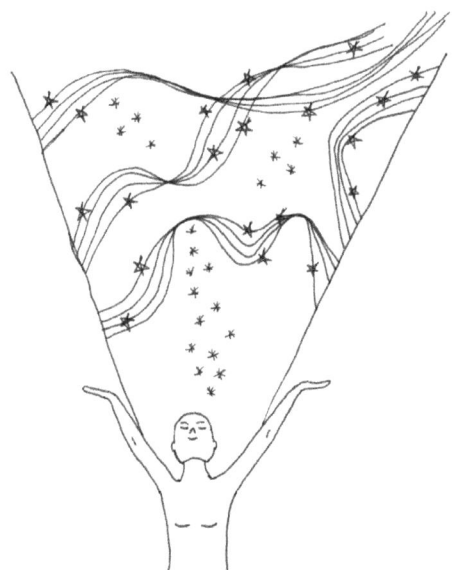

Space

A sunny field of corn
With a canopy of blue
Outer space twinkling
With stars old and new

A wide-open lake
With a tree-trimmed edge
A lush green allotment
With lots of plump veg

Nature's open spaces
Not only outside;
Move beyond your own field
Expand mind, and soul, inside

Feel your cells expanding
With big bright energy
Soaking up each and every
Speck of positivity

Expand into the distance
Feel so light and free
Density left behind
Opened up to possibility

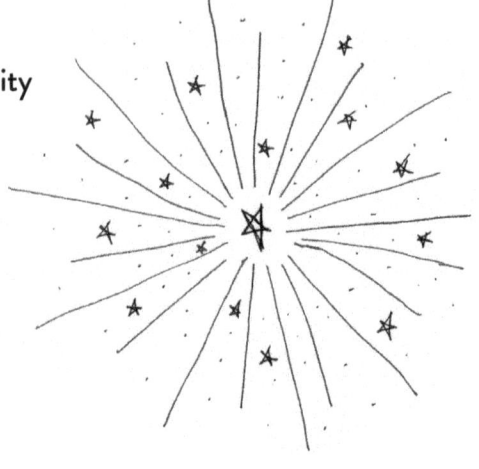

JOY

I'm too grateful to be awake
to sleep.

Soaking up spring like a big yellow sponge.

Cancer puts emotions in technicolour.

I'm shaking up and shaking
out stagnant energy.

Your First Trip to the Beach

Sea dipping
Wave tripping
Shade chasing
Wind bracing
Seaweed kicking
Shell picking
Sandy lunching
Ice-cream munching
Castle building
Spade wielding
Ball chasing
Friend making
Kisses snatching
Laughter catching

The Kingfisher

As we meandered through the park
A kingfisher emerged from the dark
A sprightly flash of vivid teal blue
Small in stature, grand in presence, too.

Delivering a beautiful moment of focus
A joyful colour burst against spring crocus
Darting across us at just the right time
Promising prosperity for the mountain we climb

Apple Crumble

The weekend ended with warm apple crumble
Golden and spicy, soft and delicious
From spoon to eager big bowls it did tumble
Dolloped yoghurt; nurturing, nutritious

Golden and spicy, soft and delicious
Apples from the garden, ripe and freshly cut
Dolloped yoghurt; nurturing, nutritious
Infused with abundant love from soil to gut

Apples from the garden, ripe and freshly cut
Wheelbarrow drop-off; veg, wild blooms in the yield
Infused with abundant love from soil to gut
All food foraged from local forest and field

Wheelbarrow drop-off; veg, wild blooms in the yield
Bustling hands all day chopping and baking
All food foraged from local forest and field
Hot water bottle bellies, hearts full and aching

Bustling hands all day chopping and baking
The weekend ended with warm apple crumble
Hot water bottle bellies, hearts full and aching
From spoon to eager big bowls it did tumble

Inspired by Jo's amazing crumble at The Retreat, 42 Acres, Somerset, UK

The Garden Centre

The air is fresh and damp. Bursts of blooms
signal summer. Crimson and candy pink
petunias nestle next to Grandma's marigolds –
little lion heads swaying in the sun.
Reliable geraniums, always 3 for £10, wait
confidently. At the other end, one-of-a-kind
palm trees and majestic clumps of golden
bamboo flex in the wind.

Garden guru titbits hum between tricky towers
of compost and alluring pots in sumptuous
emeralds and cobalts. Trolleys are tamed,
filled with horticultural hauls – who will
get the last pampas grass? Will it all fit in
the boot?

People dance around the yellow hose pipe, a
plant lifeline clumsily sashaying between
sections, leaving pop-up puddles. Relaxed
smiles vibrate in the air, as families grab
last minute pear drops at the check-out, and
friends natter over hot tea and sticky buns.

Feet rooted to earth
entwined forever as one
energies collide

The Aspen Tree

Leaves quiver above, shimmying in the sunlight
Each ripple in time swimming into the next

Golden green tongues sing their song
Secret, sacred notes spilling into the air

A rhythmic pitter-patter rings out
Seconds, minutes, moments flutter by

Take me into the breeze
Let my heart soar free
Lift me into the wild
From under the Aspen tree

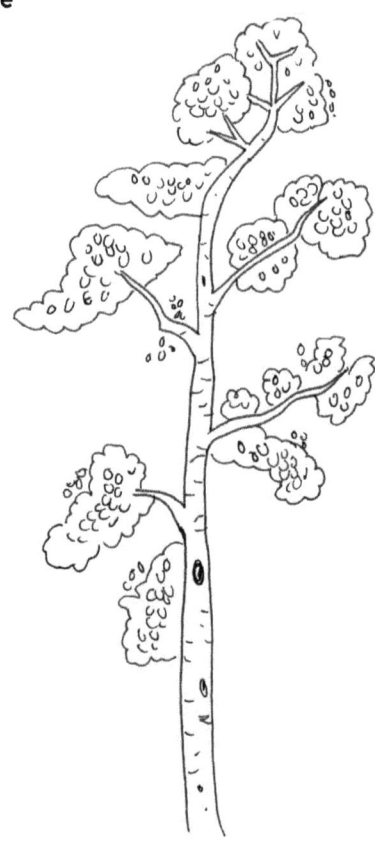

Joy

I'm ready for joy.
Kitchen dancing
Sunshine munching
Running naked in a field
Joy

Letting Go

At the end of a rainstorm
A rounded raindrop squats on a leaf
Its momentary resting place
On a vertical journey from the sky

Eventually, the raindrop surrenders
To the situation
And falls to the earth
Freely flowing into the future

The raindrop doesn't fear
The unknown or what comes next
But relinquishes control
With complete trust in the process

Pieces

I picked up
all the broken pieces
of the past
and discovered they were
treasure

Dance

And then my body became the breeze
Ribbon limbs levitating in unison with leaves

Forever

for Griff

When snowflakes kiss the tip of your nose
Or the snow crunches beneath your toes

When you walk through a lake of golden leaves
And they dance around you in the cool breeze

When a million stars shine in the sky
Or a shooting star passes you by

When the sun's warmth seeps deep to your bones
And the sea caresses sand and stones

When daffodils pop up to find the light
And lushness awakens, the air gleams bright

No matter the weather
I'm with you forever

About the Author

From Penarth, South Wales, Emily trained as a journalist before spending 15 years as a public relations and digital marketing executive in London.

Four months after becoming a mum, her life was turned upside down by a diagnosis of secondary breast cancer. Facing every stage of the journey that followed with unfaltering determination and positivity she discovered a love and talent for poetry along the way.

Not Much Rhymes with Cancer: A Collection of Healing Poems is published posthumously by her closest friends and family to whom she was, and remains, an inspiration.

More of her work can be seen on Instagram at @notmuchrhymeswithcancer.

Acknowledgements

For making this book a reality, thank you to...

Emily's husband, Lee Thomas: for being the driving force in getting this book off the ground; by rallying friends & family to get behind this project; for invaluable input and support throughout the whole production. And for believing in the power of Emily's words.

Emily's parents, Jenny and Martyn; and Emily's sisters Katie and Megan, for entrusting Emily's friends with this incredibly personal project; and for all their encouragement and advice during the book's creation.

Emily's close friends: Emily Van Keogh, Sally Cusack, Megan Merrett, Melissa Baldwin and Anna Cooke; who undertook this project from start to finish. From Sally's initiation of the crowdfunding page to raise money and awareness; to researching, collating, editing, designing and liaising with experts in the field. Over many months, this group of friends lovingly breathed life into this book, thereby helping to fulfil Emily's wishes of having her beloved poetry collection published.

Lisa Burling (Worms) – one of Emily's dearest friends – for her incredible generosity, not only with the initial fundraising for the book, but also with her invaluable guidance during the early planning stages.

Maureen Weekes at EIV publishing – already familiar with Emily and her work, Maureen gave a valuable early insight into the workings of poetry publishing. Her advice and unfaltering encouragement during the initial book discussions, inspired Emily's family and friends to begin working on the first steps.

Jamie McGarry at Valley Press for his publishing expertise, support and guidance. For his faith and belief in this book, motivating all those involved in its production; and steering it in the right direction throughout the course of its publishing journey.

Emily's sister Megan, for taking inspiration from Emily's original poetry pictures and drawing on her own artistic skills, to lovingly create beautiful new illustrations, that faithfully stayed true to Emily's vision.

Charlotte Thomas-Hui, for her creative vision, design expertise and patience in developing the book cover (in the vibrant colours Emily loved!)

Lianne Bryce and everyone at Make 2nds Count – a charity very close to Emily's heart – for cementing the partnership with this publication, and for highlighting the incredibly important work this charity does on a daily basis.

A special mention should also be given to all the wonderful people who inspired and supported Emily during her poetry journey:

Firstly, Emily's great friend Tracey Ward, who collaborated with Emily to create 'The Naked Poets': organising workshops to bring breast cancer community voices together through poetry healing; and providing an opportunity for self expression and connection.

In addition, Sarah Jane Price, a fellow writer/poet (@sjpgator) who Emily found a strong connection with: an affinity born from their mutual love for poetry, their belief in the healing power of nature, the highs and lows of their shared cancer experience, and their positive, hopeful, determined outlook on life.

To the secondary breast cancer community who, in Emily's own words, are 'right by each other's sides, every step of the way, inspiring, sharing, supporting, praying, laughing, hoping'.

Finally to Griff, whose glorious entrance into this world sparked in Emily elevated feelings of newfound love & happiness: fuelled by this experience of powerful emotions and protective instincts (that only motherhood can bring), Griff provided her with the inspiration to create some of her most beautiful, poignant and captivating works.

Giving hope to those affected by
secondary breast cancer.

Make 2nds Count is a patient and family-focused charity
dedicated to giving hope to women and men living with
secondary breast cancer. Our mission is: to fund secondary
breast cancer research that contributes to advancing an increased
quality of life for patients; establish a community that supports
and educates patients and families affected by secondary breast
cancer; inform and facilitate access to patient trials, and to
increase overall awareness of secondary breast cancer.

Secondary breast cancer, also known as metastatic, advanced or
stage IV breast cancer, is a cancer that has spread beyond the
breast to other parts of the body. Parts of the body affected are
usually the bones, liver, lungs, brain or the skin.

We hear about breast cancer on almost a daily basis. We
published research in October 2021 with YouGov – 38% of the
adult population in the UK don't know what secondary breast
cancer is even though the disease kills on average 1,000 people
every single month in the UK alone.

Secondary breast cancer can be treated but it cannot be cured.
Treatments aim to control and slow down the disease to enable
patients to have the best possible quality of life for as long as
possible.

By supporting Make 2nds Count you are helping to give hope to
everyone affected by secondary breast cancer.

Milton Keynes UK
Ingram Content Group UK Ltd.
UKHW032313161024
449556UK00002B/6

9 781915 606549